About 25 years ago I arrived in the United States of America with books in my bags for graduate studies, and zeal in my soul to explore this great land of opportunity. Today I am privileged to call this amazing country my home.

As I built my life here and learned of America's heritages, the appreciation of my own Chinese identity also grew. A sense of humor is sometimes required in order to enjoy the differences between the two cultures, I concluded. I love eating Chinese food while my American husband has trouble figuring out the calories in the dishes. Cooking I am good at, but baking is not my forte. You see, Chinese cooking is a creative process with little or no measuring involved, and baking is usually a matter of following an exact formula.

Speaking of measuring, I would rather enjoy sightseeing on a road trip than calculating the time of getting to our destination. To me, 300 miles is more or less the same as 350 miles, just as long as we GET there. I once set a goal for my life and was 10 years late getting there. You guessed it, I did not give myself a hard time.

Fish by Chu Ta, Qing Dynasty (1644-1911)

引此偏懷惟悼人緣白
亡不雨三甸雲昆明的升重兑
扡束蜀紫胃金子蓉
茫吉宋米
㞢

An interesting analogy to my life, as well as many of my Chinese friends, is the concept of "empty space" in the art of Chinese painting. See the space around the fish in this painting? That space imparts a living energy and offers the viewer an unlimited sense of possibility. This "wondrous scene" represents all the pursuits — past, present, and future — of my short life on earth.

星雷日月中火竹石水井果田眉耳齒心

The differences between Chinese and American cultures are so vast and intriguing that many scholars have written volumes about them. I do not intend to delve into an academic comparison. This companion book to **D is for Doufu** will take a closer look at the Chinese language. Perhaps we can gain more understanding as to why Chinese people are artful thinkers, and how that thinking pattern has been affecting our behavior for almost five millennia.

As you read on, you will make new discoveries about our ancient but living language, and you may draw your own conclusions as to whether learning the Chinese language is worth further pursuing. Any non-Chinese who shows interest in learning the language has my utmost respect and admiration. My love for this language deepened as I relearned its beauty while working on these two books. I sincerely hope to share this love with you.

Various legends exist to illustrate the beginning of the Chinese written language. The most credible story tells of Cāng Jíe who was a minister of the first Emperor Huáng Dì. He noticed how each animal footprint was distinct and recognizable. He was then inspired to draw the objects observed. By simplifying the number of lines in his drawings Cāng Jíe created the first pictographs.

Many objects — such as animals, plants, things of nature, and parts of the body — can be represented well with pictographs. But over time, pictographs tend to lose their resemblance to the originals, and turn into modern Chinese characters.

Object	Ancestral	Traditional	Simplified
		bèi 貝 shell	贝
		車	车
		ér 兒 child	儿
		mén 門 door	门
		龍	龙

Words from *D is for Doufu* are not romanized. See **word card** insert for more information.

Since abstract and concept words are not always visible or easy to draw, new words are formed by borrowing from pictographs. My favorite beginner's concept words are the four directions.

beǐ

北

north

xī

西

west

dōng

東

east

nán

南

south

Coinciding with the four direction words is another set of position words. When facing north to give directions, most Chinese tend to say "turn left" instead of "head west," and "go down" instead of "walk south." Anthropologists probably have a reason for this national trait of ours.

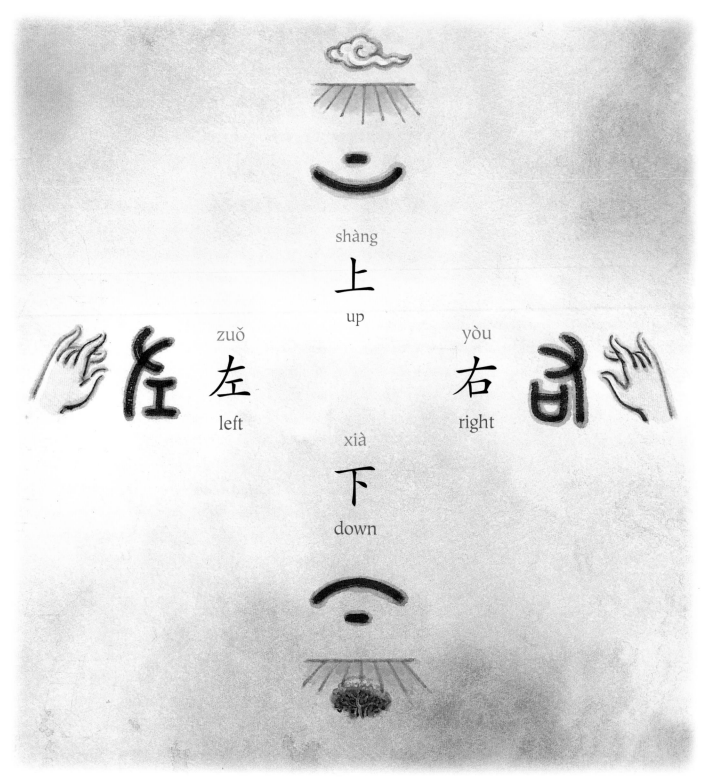

shàng

上

up

zuǒ

左

left

yòu

右

right

xià

下

down

Number words are ideographs, also. Many introductory Chinese word books include only the characters for 1 to 10, as seen below. But, by learning four more words, you can count as high as 99,999,999! Simply turn to the next page and math will never be the same again!

<u>Ancestral</u>	<u>Traditional</u>	<u>Ancestral</u>	<u>Traditional</u>
一	yī 一 one	介	liù 六 six
二	二	七	qī 七 seven
三	sān 三 three	八	bā 八 eight
四	sì 四 four	乁	jiǔ 九 nine
区	wǔ 五 five	┃	十

Words from **D is for Doufu** are not romanized. See **word card** insert for more information.

First, let's count to 99:

1 1 = 10 + 1

十 一

3 4 = 3 x 10 + 4

三 十 四

5 6 = 5 x 10 + 6

五 十 六

9 9 = 9 x 10 + 9

九 十 九

Good job! Now, here are the four powerful characters that will help you count higher.

Ancestral	Traditional	Ancestral	Traditional

líng
零
zero

qiān
千
thousand

百

wàn
萬
ten thousand

"Zero" is used only as a place holder in Chinese.

Here is how:

$101 = 1 \times 100 + 0 + 1$

一 百 零 一

$405 = 4 \times 100 + 0 + 5$

四 百 零 五

$708 = 7 \times 100 + 0 + 8$

七 百 零 八

and so on, and so on...

To really impress someone, add the word "thousand"
and count to 9,999.

$1,001 = 1 \times 1,000 + 0 + 1$

一 千 零 一

$6,789 = 6 \times 1,000 + 7 \times 100 + 8 \times 10 + 9$

六 千 七 百 八 十 九

...and you are on your own!

(Math wizards can try using the character for "10,000"
and count to 99,999,999.)

The high demand for more abstract characters for everyday living soon had our smart ancestors thinking, and a new group of characters was invented. It consisted of a determinative part (later called a radical) — usually a pictograph — conveying the meaning; and a phonetic part — usually an ideograph — giving a distinctive sound to the word. This type of word is similar to the compound words in many languages. Linguists like to call them Picto-Phonetic Characters. You and I will just stick to the term compound characters.

Using this principle, many new characters were developed. Among them many share the same sound. We call them homonyms. Here are some interesting examples:

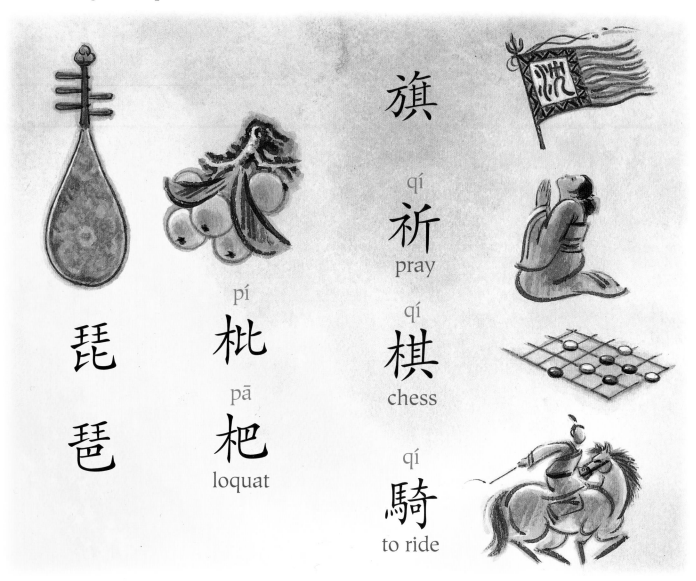

pí
枇
pā
杷
loquat

琵
琶

旗
qí
祈
pray
qí
棋
chess
qí
騎
to ride

Words from *D is for Doufu* are not romanized. See **word card** insert for more information.

Make your own red envelopes...

zhōng guó

(China)

lóng

(dragon)

shí
èr
shēng
xiào

(Chinese Horoscope)

dòu
fū

(tofu)

gōng
fū

(kungfu)

D is for Doufu
An Alphabet Book of Chinese Culture
©1997

SHEN'S
BOOKS

800-456-6660
www.shens.com

D is for Doufu
An Alphabet Book of Chinese Culture
©1997

SHEN'S
BOOKS

800-456-6660
www.shens.com

D is for Doufu
An Alphabet Book of Chinese Culture
©1997

SHEN'S
BOOKS

800-456-6660
www.shens.com

D is for Doufu
An Alphabet Book of Chinese Culture
©1997

SHEN'S
BOOKS

800-456-6660
www.shens.com

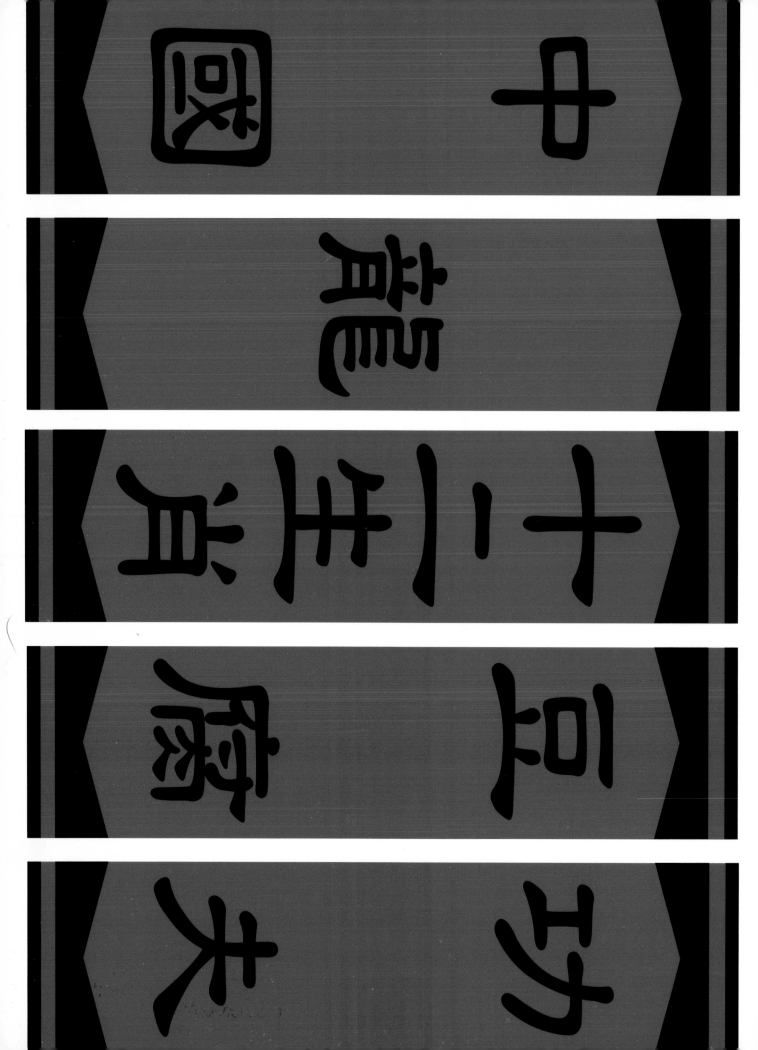

ài	bǎi	jiā	xìng
愛	百	家	姓
love	hundred	home	surname

chē	dòu	fǔ	ēn
車	豆	腐	恩
vehicle	bean	ferment	kindness

fēng	shuǐ	gōng	fū
風	水	功	夫
wind	water	effort	adult male

hóng	bāo	jià	qǔ
紅	包	嫁	娶
red	wrap, bag	marry into	marry

kuaì	zi	lóng	má
筷	子	龍	麻
chopstick	child	dragon	flax, numb

jìang	nào	huā	dēng
將	鬧	花	燈
a general	make noise	flower	lamp

There are 23 terms introduced in **D is for Doufu**, which total 42 individual words. Each word is called a character.

All 42 characters are listed on this spread with *Hanyu Pinyin* (romanized Chinese) in red to help you sound out the words.

The part printed in green represents a radical. See page 12-14 for more information.

The squares can be cut out and used as word cards to do some of the exercises in this book.

You can also make word cards for the new words your learn from this book and design your own games. Number words are the most fun to play with. See if you can count to 99,999,999 with only 14 characters! Page 7-9 will help you get started.

oǔ 藕 lotus root	pí 琵 string instrument	pā 琶 string instrument
qí 旗 banner	páo 袍 robe	rěn 忍 patience
shí 十 ten	èr 二 two	shēng 生 life, give birth
xìao 肖 animal	tú 圖 picture	zhāng 章 chop, seal
wǒ 我 I, me	xìao 孝 of filial piety	shùn 順 obedient
yù 玉 jade	zhōng 中 center, middle	guó 國 country

免水自貼膠口

SHEN'S BOOKS
800 - 456 - 6660

免水自貼膠口

SHEN'S BOOKS
800 - 456 - 6660

The most interesting homonyms, in my opinion, are in my own name—Shen Maywan.

shěn
沈
Surname

shěn
審
to question

méi
眉
eyebrow

méi
沒
no

wán
紈
white silk

wán
完
end

So, when in doubt, always ask a Chinese how his name is written. Knowing how to say his name is good indeed, but knowing what each character represents is truly impressive. Besides, you will learn the story behind the person's name, be it genealogical, in memory of, or for luck, it will definitely help you remember the person's name. To many of my friends, I am sometimes like a "Never-Ending Question," or so they think.

We have already learned that once a pictograph is chosen to be the determinative part of a word, it is called a radical. It always indicates the original intent of the word. This system was mainly devised for classification in a dictionary. The current number of radicals is 214. Out of the 42 individual characters in **D is for Doufu**, we find only 20 radicals. They are highlighted on the word cards (see insert). Can you match some of them with the list below?

Radical	Meaning			
女	female	姓	嫁	娶
子	child	孝		
卄	plant	花	藕	
心	heart	愛	恩	忍
力	strength	功	yǒng 勇 brave	
火	fire	chǎo 燈	炒 stirfry	

FUN WITH RADICALS

This Mix-and-Match exercise will give you a better idea of the function of a radical. Here are some interesting examples using familiar radicals with unfamiliar parts.

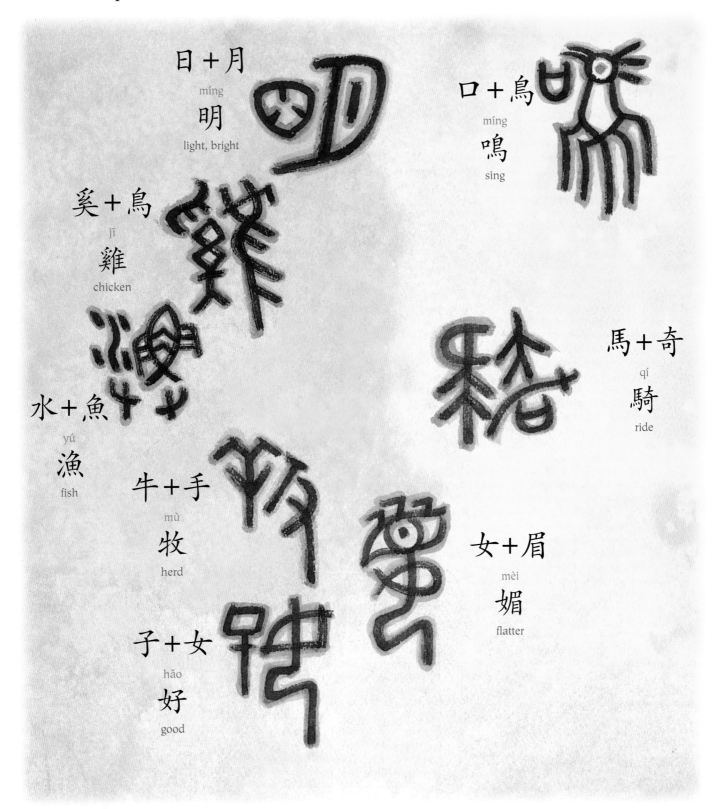

日＋月
míng
明
light, bright

口＋鳥
míng
鳴
sing

奚＋鳥
jī
雞
chicken

水＋魚
yú
漁
fish

馬＋奇
qí
騎
ride

牛＋手
mù
牧
herd

女＋眉
mèi
媚
flatter

子＋女
hǎo
好
good

An exciting thing happened when our forefathers repeated a radical once, or twice to form a new word, in order to emphasize or enhance an idea. 轟 is listed in **D is for Doufu** to get you started. Let's see what other "pile-ups" we can concoct together.

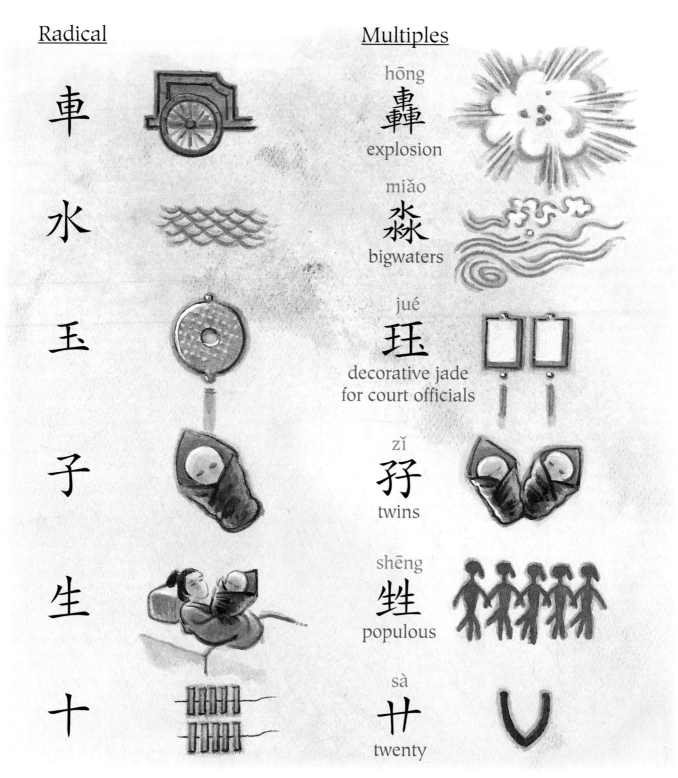

Radical | Multiples

車

水

玉

子

生

十

hōng
轟
explosion

miǎo
淼
bigwaters

jué
珏
decorative jade
for court officials

zǐ
孖
twins

shēng
甡
populous

sà
廿
twenty

Words from **D is for Doufu** are not romanized. See **word card** insert for more information.

Chinese regard the human heart as the source of all feelings, values, and morals. Using "heart" as a radical, numerous words have been devised. I will name a few to illustrate the wisdom of Chinese writing.

Chinese characters are written within the framework of a square. Auxiliary lines are provided in handwriting workbooks to help beginners until one can master the art of "writing within the lines."

Each character is made up of one or more parts, and here are some basic structures.

Form   Examples

紅   順   燈

家   忍   孝

鬧

愛   腐   車   章

藕   筷   花

As a school kid, I spent hours each day learning and practicing the placement of each stroke, column after column, row after row. As a result, I developed my own style of writing. Even after 20 years of living apart from the mainstream Chinese, I can still read and write the language. As for my penmanship, I admit, it can use some improvement.

As the previous page shows, writing Chinese is like drawing in a square. Always start from the top or upper left corner and work your way down or toward the lower right corner. This way you follow the natural sequence of the strokes and can write smoothly and quickly.

Each line drawn in a Chinese character is called a stroke. There are 9 basic strokes.

Name of Stroke	Stroke	Example		
horizontal	一	玉	豆	
vertical	丨	中	車	
sweep to the left	丿	夫	花	肖
sweep to the right	乀	筷	水	
dot	丶	家	恩	
upward stroke	一	功	子	
hook (left or right)	亅乀	我	袍	國
horizontal turn	フ	百		
vertical turn	ㄴ	琵		

The all-time favorite example of the types of strokes is the word "forever."

yǒng

永

It comprises **eight** major strokes.

Ideas begin to form when you put words together. Join two or more characters and you have the forerunner of a term, a phrase, or a sentence. **D is for Doufu** has 23 terms, many of which can be rearranged to give birth to new ideas. Let's try it on the color word "red".

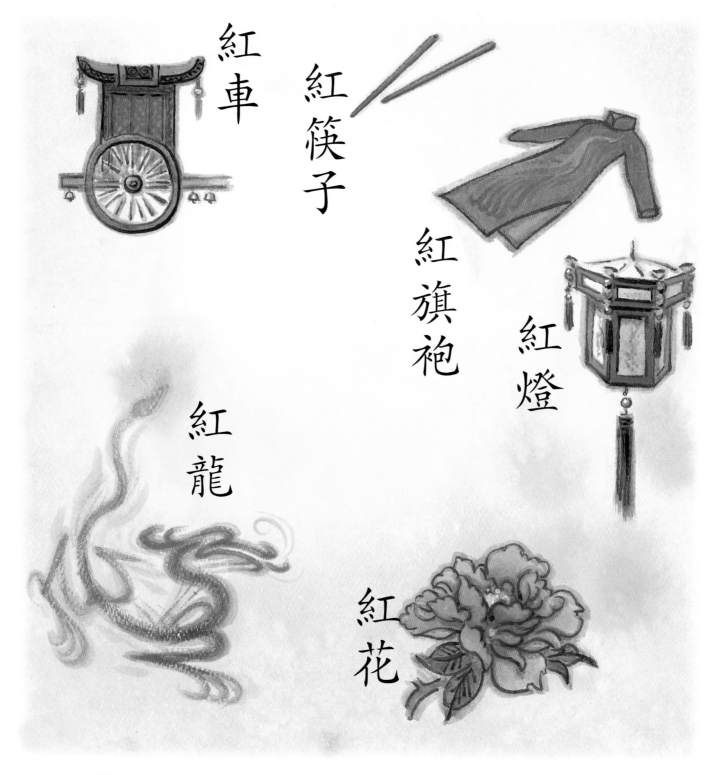

紅車

紅筷子

紅旗袍

紅燈

紅龍

紅花

Words from **D is for Doufu** are not romanized. See **word card** insert for more information.

A complete thought is born by adding a subject and a verb to a term you put together. To wrap up our lesson it seems proper to use the auspicious word "dragon" to demonstrate how you can read and write a complete sentence in Chinese!

龍

我生龍子

龍子

龍

龍袍

我愛龍袍

我愛美國

我愛中國

měi
美
beautiful